D0239034

DREAMS
and *sleep*

Trudi Strain Trueit

Franklin Watts
A Division of Scholastic Inc.
New York • Toronto • London • Auckland • Sydney
Mexico City • New Delhi • Hong Kong
Danbury, Connecticut

Dedication

For Kensie—May you always follow your faith,
your heart, and your dreams.

Cover design by Robert O'Brien.
Interior design by Kathleen Santini.
Illustration p. 10 by Mike DiGiorgio.
Photographs p. 22 © 2004 James Holmes / Photo Researchers, Inc. /
 Science Photo Library.

Library of Congress Cataloging-in-Publication Data

Trueit, Trudi Strain.
  Dreams and Sleep / Trudi Strain Trueit.
    p. cm. — (Life balance)
Summary: Examines the science of sleep, including what happens
when we sleep, how much sleep we need, sleep problems, and
the connection between sleep and dreams, and provides an in-
troduction to dream interpretation.
Includes bibliographical references and index.
  ISBN 0-531-12260-3 (lib. bdg.)   0-531-15579-X (pbk.)
  1. Sleep—Juvenile literature. 2. Dreams—Juvenile literature.
[1. Sleep. 2. Dreams] I. Title: Dreams and sleep. II. Title. III. Series.
  QP425.T785 2004
  612.8'21—dc21
                              2003005829

Table of Contents

Introduction
Tapestry
of Dreams

Did you dream last night?

Actually, that's a trick question, because everyone must answer "yes." Every person dreams every single night. A dream is like a tapestry, as individual and unique as its weaver—you! While you sleep, your brain remains active, sewing together a collage of your memories, problems, wishes, and goals. Perhaps your dream tapestry is woven in threads of black and white, or maybe you dream in color. Many of the sensations you feel during your waking hours give texture to your nightly masterpiece. Did you have mashed potatoes for dinner? Are you painting your room purple? Don't be surprised to find yourself dreaming of floating on a fluffy mashed-potato cloud across a lavender sky. Your imagination may come alive as well, creating stories and characters to add dimension to your dreams. Dream experts say that we typically have about four to five dream sequences each night—that amounts to nearly 140,000 dreams during the average person's lifetime. Therefore, maybe a better question to begin this book might be *what* did you dream last night? Don't worry if you can't remember. Most of us recall only small fragments of the various images that dance within our heads during slumber.

In *Dreams and Sleep,* we'll journey into the mysterious world that awaits us just beyond the sunset. We'll explore how your nightly tapestries take shape and show you how to better recollect them. You'll discover what your dreams may be trying to tell you as you learn to keep your own dream journal. However, before we can begin to unlock our dreams, we need to understand their launching point: sleep. Kids spend, on average, about 40 percent of their time sleeping. Yet, did you ever give much thought to what you devote so much of your life to doing? In this book, you'll learn why everything you do, from kicking a soccer ball to playing a musical instrument, depends on getting a good night's rest. Your nightly dreams, too, rely on healthy sleep patterns. We'll see the tragic consequences that can occur when people don't get enough sleep and show you ways to make sound sleeping habits part of your life.

So read on, sleep well, and sweet dreams!

Part One
Sleep

One

Slumber Science

t is a clear, starry night—perfect for enjoying a late summer meteor shower. Lying back on a patch of grass you gaze up into a sapphire sky. You search the heavens for a streak of fiery sparks made by space dust burning up as it enters Earth's atmosphere. For a while, you fend off drowsiness by whistling and jiggling your feet. Eventually, though, your body's insistence upon rest wins out over your desire to remain awake. This is just as nature intended it to be. Lulled by a gentle breeze, you fall asleep under the stars and awaken the next morning. This pattern, called the sleep-wake cycle, continues day after day for your entire life. In fact, you will spend more than one-third of your life "catching some z's."

Sleep is a state of partial or full unconsciousness from which you can be awakened. It is characterized by changes in the body and brain. When you sleep, you close your eyes and lie fairly still. Muscles relax, breathing slows, and heart rate and body temperature gradually fall. Soon you are no longer aware of your surroundings. Although scientists are still unraveling the mystery of why we need to sleep, they have discovered that the hours we spend in slumber can dramatically affect how we function while we're awake.

Healthy Snooze

Studies show that sick people sleep twice as much as those who are healthy. Sleep gives the immune system a chance to spend all its energy battling the virus. Research has also found that ill people who don't get enough sleep take longer to recover. So the next time you have a cold or flu, make sure you get plenty of rest.

Studies show that during the deepest part of sleep, cells in the body are repairing, reproducing, and reenergizing for the day ahead. Human growth hormone, a natural chemical produced by the body, is released to aid in the development of cells and tissues. It also helps mend the body by fighting infection and healing cuts and bruises. During deep sleep, the area of the brain that controls decision-making and social skills shows a decrease in activity.

Scientists say dreaming is an important element of the sleep-wake cycle, allowing the mind to sort out events, issues, and memories.

This has led some scientists to conclude that deep sleep gives neurons—brain cells that relay nerve messages within the brain and central nervous system—a chance to repair and establish new connections. Yet, when we reach the point in sleep where we begin to dream, the brain becomes very active. Scientists say dreaming is an important element of the sleep-wake cycle, allowing the mind to sort out events, issues, and memories.

Your Body Clock Is Ticking

Did you ever wonder how your body knows when to sleep and when to wake up? The answer lies in an area of your brain called the SCN, short for suprachiasmatic nucleus. The SCN, located in the hypothalamus, is the control center for many bodily functions, including the sleep-wake cycle, hormone levels, heart rate, blood pressure, and body temperature. The SCN is often referred to as your biological clock, or body clock. Because the natural functions controlled by your body clock follow a predictable daily routine, they are known as circadian rhythms. "Circadian" comes from the Latin *circa dies,* meaning "about a day."

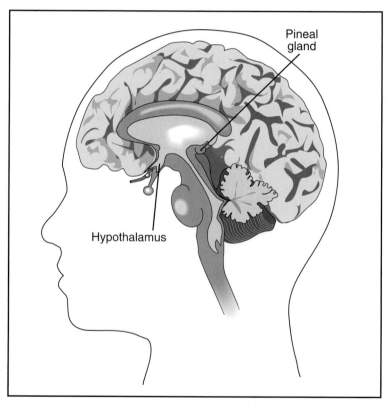

The SCN is located in the hypothalamus. The main function of the hypothalamus is to regulate certain bodily functions, such as blood pressure and body temperature.

Your body clock controls the sleep-wake cycle by releasing certain chemicals at certain times of the day. These chemicals act as signals to your body, telling you when to sleep and when you've had enough rest. For instance, our body clocks typically wind down a bit after lunch, between 1:00 and 4:00 P.M., and again in the early morning between 1:00 and 4:00 A.M. These are the hours we tend to feel the least alert.

The body clock also takes its cues from the sun. As the first inkling of sunlight hits the back of your eyes in the morning, messages are sent along the optic nerves to

Beyond the Winter Blues

The Mayo Clinic estimates that somewhere between 6 million and 30 million people in the United States suffer from seasonal affective disorder (SAD), a condition in which those who aren't exposed to enough sunlight become severely depressed. SAD frequently occurs in late fall as the amount of daylight decreases and clouds are more apt to block sunlight. Therapy involves sitting in front of a high-intensity light box for a few hours each day or creating a "fake dawn" where the patient slowly awakens to an artificial light on dark winter mornings. Usually, SAD lifts naturally in the springtime when daylight hours lengthen and the sun shines more often.

the SCN. The SCN then tells the pineal gland, a pea-size organ located nearby in the brain, to stop producing melatonin. Melatonin is a hormone, a natural chemical produced by the body, that helps regulate your sleep cycle. Gradually, you awaken from slumber. At the end of the day, as darkness falls, the SCN notes the decrease in light. The pineal gland is alerted to increase the flow of melatonin, which tells the brain and body that it's getting dark and that it's time to get ready for sleep. The body clock is continually adjusting itself in response to the amount of sunlight it receives. That is why in the summer, when there are more hours of sunlight in the day, you naturally wake up earlier and have extra energy to stay up later.

In teenagers, hormonal changes that occur in puberty may cause the pineal gland to release melatonin later in the evening than usual. This shift can dramatically affect a teen's sleep-wake cycle, leading to a disorder called delayed sleep phase syndrome. In a National Sleep Foundation article, "Dozing Off in Class?", Dr. Mary Carskadon, director of the Sleep Research Lab at Bradley Hospital in Providence, Rhode Island, explains the problem. "Many adolescents are physiologically not ready to fall asleep until 11:00 P.M. or later. The average teen needs about nine hours of sleep, but many students sleep less than seven hours, in part because they need to get to school by

7:30 A.M. As a result, many teens experience problem sleepiness during the day."

In 1997, recognizing that sleep deprivation was having a serious impact on students, the school district of Minneapolis, Minnesota, moved its high-school start times from 7:15 A.M. to 8:40 A.M. Studies found that the extra sleep helped boost mood, memory, and grades, while lowering absentee and tardy rates. Almost 60 percent of teachers noticed that the students in their morning classes were much more alert when school started later. Many school districts across the country are now following this example, opting to shift to a later schedule so students can arrive well rested for the day.

If you routinely feel more energetic and productive in the earliest part of the day, then you would be considered a morning person or "lark." If you are more alert and active in the evening, then you are most likely a night person or an "owl."

Your biological clock also determines whether you are a morning person or a night person. If you routinely feel more energetic and productive in the earliest part of the day, then you would be considered a morning person or "lark." A meadowlark is a type of blackbird that sings in the morning hours.

Psst ... Are You Asleep?

All birds, mammals, and reptiles sleep, but there is debate about whether other types of animals—such as insects, invertebrates, and fish—actually fall asleep or merely rest. Research has found that the amount of sleep necessary to maintain health and energy varies from species to species. Nocturnal animals, those that sleep during the day and awaken at night, need the most rest. Opossums, bats, armadillos, and sloths may spend eighteen or more hours a day (about 80 percent of their lives) snoozing. Yet, large mammals like elephants, horses, and deer require less than four hours of sleep per day.

Fascinating Sleep Habits

Animal	Amount of Sleep Needed in 24 Hours	Did You Know...?
Bat	20 hours	A bat sleeps hanging upside down. Special tendons in its feet lock the toes to a cave wall or tree branch. The bat must flex its muscles to let go.

Animal	Amount of Sleep Needed in 24 Hours	Did You Know...?
Sloth	18 hours	A sloth will spend virtually its entire life in a tree—sleeping, eating, mating, and giving birth clinging upside down to a branch in the rain forest.
Cat	15 hours	Most cats dream about every 15 minutes. If your cat's paws, ears, or whiskers are twitching while asleep, the cat is probably dreaming.
Dolphin	7 hours	Dolphins and some types of birds have unihemispheric brains: one half of the brain remains awake while the other half sleeps. This allows dolphins to slumber as they swim and many seabirds to nap in flight.
Blue jay	5 hours	Perching birds, like jays, pigeons, and chickadees, sleep standing up. Muscles in their legs and claws go rigid to keep them from falling off tree branches.
Giraffe	20 minutes	Giraffes may sleep standing or lying down, though they rarely rest for more than 5 to 10 minutes at a time.

On the other hand, if you are more alert and active in the evening, then you are most likely a night person or an "owl," named for the bird of prey that sleeps during the day and hunts at night. Studies have found that our genetic makeup is what decides whether we are larks or owls. So, chances are, you can thank your parents for setting your body clock.

Sleep Requirements

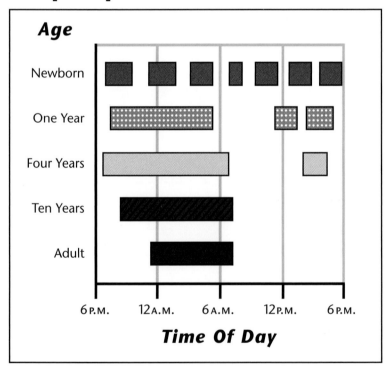

As children develop, both the distribution of sleep in a 24-hour period and total sleep requirements change.

Adult humans usually require between seven and nine hours of sleep to function at their best. Scientists have yet to discover exactly how much sleep kids need at different stages of childhood, but, generally, the younger a person is, the more sleep he or she should have. While sixteen to twenty hours of sleep a day is necessary for babies, preschoolers need thirteen to fifteen hours, and elementary-school kids should have ten to twelve hours of sleep. Children over age ten and teenagers should shoot for between nine and ten hours of sleep per night.

While You Are *Sleeping*

Two

Try to remember the very moment you fell asleep last night. Having trouble? You might be able to recall what you were thinking a few minutes before you nodded off, but you probably cannot recollect the *exact* instant it occurred. Scientists compare falling asleep to turning off a light switch. One moment the switch is on, the next it's off. One second you are awake, the next you're asleep. But that doesn't mean that your brain stops functioning during sleep.

Scientists have found that our brains are constantly giving off tiny electrical charges we cannot feel, even during sleep. These currents are indicators of the kind of activity going on inside the brain. Researchers rely on a device called an electroencephalograph, or EEG, to record these electrical currents. Up to twenty small metal electrodes are attached to the scalp using easily removable glue or tape. The electrodes detect the tiny electrical impulses released by nerve cells. Wires relay the information to an EEG machine, which increases the size of the signals so they can be digitally read by a computer. The patterns of squiggly lines that are mapped by an EEG are known as brain waves, and the written record of brain waves is called an electroencephalogram. EEGs are valuable tools used in diagnosing tumors, strokes, epilepsy, sleep disorders, and infections of the brain such as multiple sclerosis.

Sleeping Too Deeply

A coma is a state of sleep from which a person cannot be awakened. The EEG of someone in a coma shows brain waves that are slow and barely detectable. Bleeding in the brain, drug overdose, viral infection, or lack of oxygen are some of the things that can cause a dramatic decrease in brain activity, which can lead to a coma.

The Sleep Cycle

It is only within the past sixty years, with the advent of the EEG, that scientists have discovered that we produce distinctive brain waves while we are asleep. These patterns change throughout the night, revealing that we pass through five separate stages during sleep. Together, these stages are known as the sleep cycle.

Drowsing: You are dozing off and just beginning to fall asleep. As you drift in and out of consciousness, your muscles relax, your body temperature drops, and your heart rate and breathing slows. While drowsing, you can be easily awakened by the sound of a television or someone nudging you. You may also experience muscle contractions called hypnic jerks. Your legs or arms may jump as if you've been startled or are falling off the bed. Your brain activity slows to produce what are called alpha waves. Alpha waves are different from the waves your brain makes when you are awake, which are known as beta waves. An active brain produces tinier, quicker waves so beta waves show up as small, rapid squiggles on an EEG. In contrast, alpha waves are larger with more spikes. You stay in the dozing stage for a short time, usually less than ten minutes.

Stages One and Two: If you aren't awakened from dozing, you will move into light sleep. In this phase, you are likely to sleep through louder noises, such as a barking dog or music from a stereo. It becomes more difficult to wake you. During light sleep, your brain produces slower, deeper waves called theta waves. In stage two, theta waves may be punctured by bursts of rapid waves called sleep spindles as well as K-complexes, large waves that last for just a brief second. Light sleep lasts about ten minutes.

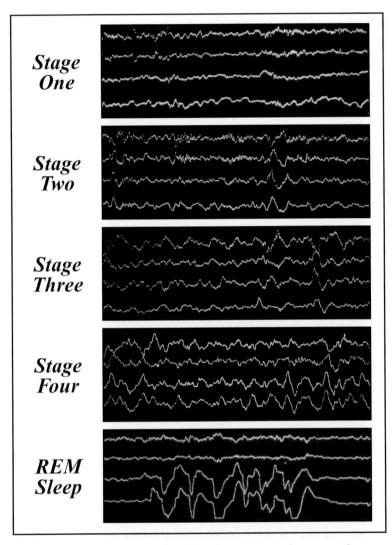

Stage One

Stage Two

Stage Three

Stage Four

REM Sleep

The first two traces in each of the sleep stages above are electro-encephalograms (EEG's), which measure brain activity. The third and fourth traces measure activity in the right and left eye.

Stages Three and Four: You have now reached what is referred to as deep sleep. You have no eye or muscle movement. Blood pressure, heart rate, and metabolism (chemical reactions that burn energy) continue to decline. Body temperature drops to its lowest point of the day. Brain activity also decreases. Deep sleep is also called slow-wave sleep due to the large, rolling brain waves that are produced on an EEG. These are called delta waves. Stages three and four are so similar that scientists usually group them together. Stage three is reached when delta waves make up 20 to 50 percent of a thirty-second time period, known as an epoch. When delta waves comprise more than 50 percent of an epoch, you have entered stage four.

Scientists conclude that it is during deep sleep that your body gets the kind of thorough rest it needs to recharge, grow, and repair. During this phase, the body releases human growth hormone necessary for cell growth, development, and fighting infection. If awakened during stages three and four you will be extremely groggy. It will take you several minutes to fully awaken. Deep sleep usually lasts for about forty-five minutes. You slowly come out of slow-wave sleep and stir as if about to awaken. But you do not wake up. Instead, you move into a very different kind of sleep.

REM Sleep: In this final stage of the sleep cycle, your heart rate, blood pressure, and metabolism start to rise. Your breathing rate and metabolism increase. Your brain becomes more active, producing brain waves similar to the beta waves that occur while you're awake. You begin what is called rapid eye movement, or REM. Beneath closed eyelids, your eyes dart quickly back and forth. REM indicates that you are actively dreaming, creating images to watch on your own private movie screen on the back of your eyelids. Your first dream cycle of the night lasts for less than ten minutes.

Brain Freeze

Do you ever wonder why when you dream of raiding the fridge you don't wake up with your head in a bowl of potato salad? Normally, when you are awake your brain sends signals to your body, which responds with movement. But during REM sleep these messages are blocked, essentially paralyzing your body so you cannot act out your dreams. (Sleepwalking and night terrors occur during slow-wave sleep, not REM sleep, so people with these disorders are not responding to their dreams.) If you've ever tried to wake up but couldn't seem to open your eyes or move your body, you probably awakened before your REM cycle was complete. It can be a scary experience, but don't panic. The paralysis that protects your body during REM sleep gradually wears off as you begin to awaken.

It takes about ninety minutes to go through one entire sleep cycle. You will repeat the loop about five times before finally waking in the morning. Scientists classify the first four

Research has shown that if people don't get enough deep sleep, they will feel tired the next day no matter how much time they have spent in the other stages of sleep.

stages of sleep as non-REM sleep. As the night progresses, your non-REM sleep becomes shorter and lighter, while each REM period lasts a little longer. Your final REM period may go on for a half hour or more. Also, it will most likely contain the dream you will remember in the morning. Over the course of a night, your total "dream time" may add up to two or three hours. Scientists say most of us spend about 80 percent of the night in non-REM sleep and about 20 percent in REM sleep.

Getting the right balance of non-REM and REM sleep is important. Research has shown that if people don't get enough deep sleep, they will feel tired the next day no matter how much time they have spent in the other stages of sleep. Likewise, studies indicate that lack of REM sleep contributes to problems with memory, mood, and concentration.

Sleep scientists say we often tend to underestimate the importance of sleep. We may think we can handle less shut-eye without suffering any ill effects, yet that is not always the case. Read on to explore more about the power of slumber and to discover the tragic consequences that can occur when people don't get enough sleep.

Three

A Good Night's
Rest

American inventor Thomas Edison, who patented more than 1,300 inventions, believed that sleep was a waste of time. "For myself, I never found need of more than four or five hours of sleep in the twenty-four," he once wrote. Edison hoped that his invention of the lightbulb would encourage people to stay up longer, be more productive, and, eventually, eliminate sleep altogether.

Edison may have gotten his wish or, at least part of it. Today, adults sleep about seven hours a night on average—two hours less than they did before the dawn of the lightbulb. The advent of artificial light created shift work, the ability for businesses to operate round-the-clock by scheduling workers to come in during the day or at night. Of course, we've hardly done away with sleep as Edison had envisioned. But with ever-increasing schedules, longer work hours, and shift work, we appear to be bent on reducing how much time we spend in slumber.

Studies show that only about 15 percent of American teens sleep more than eight and a half hours. A National Sleep Foundation survey revealed that 60 percent of kids and teens admitted they often felt very tired during the day. Being tired means you feel listless, lack energy, and aren't motivated to participate in your usual activities. This is different from being sleepy, which leads you to actually doze off during the day. In the same poll, 15 percent of kids told their parents they had fallen asleep at school at least once in the past year. Lack of sufficient sleep, called sleep deprivation, may affect your mood, concentration, and performance.

How can you make sure you are getting plenty of rest? By practicing what is known as "good sleep hygiene," advises Dr. Jodi Mindell, associate professor of psychology at St. Joseph's University in Philadelphia, Pennsylvania. "Go to bed at the same time each night and wake up at about the same time every morning. Figure out what time you have to get up in the morning then count backward nine to ten hours. Avoid caffeine," she says, "and really pay attention to this because things like coffee, ice cream, iced tea, and some

Sleepless in San Diego

In January 1964, high-school student Randy Gardner decided to submit an entry to the San Diego Science Fair. He would go without sleep for 264 hours, beating the old *Guinness Book of World Records'* time of 260 hours. When sleep researchers at the nearby United States Navy base heard about Randy's vigil, they offered to monitor him for safety and to learn more about sleep deprivation.

By the second day of the experiment, the seventeen-year-old was having trouble focusing his eyes. Three days without sleep and Randy was quick to get angry, had trouble with coordination, and struggled to repeat simple tongue twisters. By the fourth day, he was hallucinating and thought he was a famous football player. On the ninth day, Randy could no longer finish his sentences, had lapses in short-term memory, and was losing his vision. Despite his deteriorating condition, Randy made it the full 264 hours.

Perhaps what most amazed researchers was Randy's ability to bounce back so quickly after eleven days without sleep. After the experiment ended, Randy went home and slept for more than fourteen hours. When he awoke, his hallucinations were gone, and his speech, vision, and coordination had returned to normal. Experts advise never to try this on your own because it is too risky. Even sleep researchers do not conduct sleep-deprivation studies on humans because of the danger involved.

orange sodas contain caffeine. Also, sleep in a room that's cool and quiet. Avoid watching television the last half hour before you go to bed."

Have you ever found yourself tossing and turning, unable to fall asleep? Most of us have had, on occasion, a restless night or two. We count sheep or try to relax, but it's as if the more we try to fall asleep the harder it becomes. Difficulty falling or staying asleep is called insomnia. The word *insomnia* is Latin for "sleepless." Stress, illness, caffeine, or eating or exercising too close to bedtime are some things that can make it hard to get to sleep. Usually, insomnia disappears naturally in a day or two. Yet, one in ten people suffer from prolonged insomnia. If you're having trouble sleeping for more than a couple of weeks or if it is affecting your ability to function during the day, check with your doctor. It may be a symptom of a more serious problem called a sleep disorder (see p. 33).

Going into Debt

It isn't uncommon to stay up late for a night or two, and then "catch up" on sleep by snoozing for a few extra hours on the weekend. Sometimes, though, skimping on a good night's rest here and there can add up to a lot of lost sleep. This creates what is called sleep debt. Sleep debt is the difference between the amount of sleep your body needs to feel well rested and the amount of sleep you actually get. The more sleep you lose, the more your sleep debt grows.

Say you need nine hours of sleep to be at your best. If you only get seven hours of rest each night for five days, your total sleep debt for the week is ten hours—that's a whole night's sleep! Eventually, your body is going to require that your sleep debt be paid. "You might not need to repay all of your sleep debt hour for hour, but you will have to catch up on much of it," says Dr. Judith Owens, director of the Pediatric Sleep Disorders Clinic at Hasbro Children's Hospital in Providence, Rhode Island. "Sleep debt affects your attention span, concentration, reaction time, memory, and higher-level creativity."

Open Wide!

Yawning is more than an outward signal that you're bored or sleepy. It's your body's way of waking you up. When you're sleepy your breathing rate tends to slow down, and a yawn helps pump more oxygen to the brain. This gives your brain the quick boost it needs to keep you alert and functioning properly. Of course, no one knows why yawning appears to be contagious. The next time you yawn, look around and see how many people around you are, suddenly, yawning, too.

In a National Sleep Foundation poll, 37 percent of those surveyed said lack of sleep interfered with their ability to function for several days or more each month. Worse yet, because sleep debt impairs judgment, those who are affected may be unaware of how little sleep they are actually getting. They may be placing themselves and others at risk.

Accidents caused by lack of sleep are to blame for 250,000 deaths and 2.5 million disabling injuries every year. The National Highway Traffic Safety Administration reports that, each year, drivers nodding off behind the wheel cause more than 100,000 car accidents, resulting in 70,000 injuries and about 1,500 deaths. A national survey reported that half of all American adults, especially young men, admitted to driving while sleepy. One in five people confessed they *have* actually fallen asleep at the wheel.

Drowsy drivers, and anyone else who is sleep deprived, may experience what are called microsleeps. This is where a person briefly falls asleep. A microsleep can last for a few seconds up to several minutes. Slipping into a microsleep for even an instant may be all it takes for a tractor trailer to cross the centerline of a highway or a night-shift factory worker to lose control of a forklift. Scientists figure that sleep deprivation and other sleep problems cost the United States $35 billion per year in accidents and absenteeism.

Uncovering Sleep Disorders

Everyone has trouble falling asleep once in a while. However, when a problem with sleep becomes persistent or spills over to affect how someone functions during the day, it is called a sleep disorder. Scientists have identified more than eighty different sleep disorders that interfere with the delicate balance of the sleep-wake cycle. Some of the most common sleep disorders found in children include sleepwalking, night terrors, and obstructive sleep apnea.

Sleepwalking occurs when a person is caught between the stages of deep sleep and REM sleep. It usually occurs between one and three hours after going to sleep. The disorder causes the sleeper to sit up and, perhaps, move around. Most of the time, sleepwalkers don't realize what they are doing and can be quietly led back to bed. About 30 percent of all kids have sleepwalked at least once in their lives. Experts say people who do not get an adequate amount of sleep each night are at a higher risk for sleepwalking. Why? Because lack of sleep has a direct effect on the overall quality of sleep you do get. A person who is sleep deprived spends more time in deep sleep than someone who gets the proper amount of rest. The longer a person remains in deep sleep, the greater the likelihood of experiencing many of the sleep problems that occur during stages three and four, such as sleepwalking or night terrors.

The Fatigue Factor

Some of the most tragic accidents in history are the result of sleep deprivation. Although lack of sleep wasn't the only cause of the following disasters, evidence shows it was a major contributor.

Challenger space shuttle—January 28, 1986
Seventy-three seconds after it lifted off from Cape Canaveral, Florida, the space shuttle exploded. The crew of seven was killed, including the first teacher in space, Christa McAuliffe. The accident was blamed on a faulty O-ring, a sealant in a solid rocket booster. During the two months prior to the launch, NASA ground crews and scientists were working twelve-hour days for two-week stretches with no time off. In a meeting the night before the launch, sleep-deprived scientists had plenty of documentation from the O-ring's manufacturer to spot the problem. Yet, they overlooked the information and approved the launch.

Chernobyl nuclear power plant—April 26, 1986
A crew who had just been rotated to the night shift began routine safety tests in the early morning hours at one of the largest nuclear power plants in Ukraine. When a heating problem cropped up in one of the reactors, the groggy workers didn't catch it. When they finally did, they accidentally turned the emergency cooling system off instead of on. The reactor exploded, sending a plume

of radioactive gas over 2,000 square miles (3,200 square kilometers). More than seventeen million people were contaminated. A half million people died of burns and radioactive poisoning in the worst nuclear power plant accident in history.

Exxon Valdez—March 24, 1989

Just after midnight, the *Exxon Valdez* oil tanker ran aground in Alaska's Prince William Sound. At the time of the crash, the third mate at the helm was working overtime. He'd had only six hours sleep in the previous two days, far less than regulations required. When the third mate ordered the tanker be turned into the shipping lane, he failed to notice he had not taken her off autopilot. Even after crew members on deck alerted him that the lights marking the reef were on the wrong side of the ship, he still did not realize anything was wrong. By the time the third mate caught the problem, the ship was taken off automatic pilot, but it was too late. The *Exxon Valdez* couldn't make the turn and slammed into rock. Over the next few days, eleven million gallons of crude oil spilled into the bay. Wildlife officials estimate more than 250,000 seabirds, 2,800 sea otters, 250 bald eagles, and countless small animals died struggling to escape the black ooze. The *Exxon Valdez* disaster killed more wildlife than any other oil spill in U.S. history.

Night terrors are not nightmares, though the two are often confused. Nightmares occur during REM, or dream, sleep. Night terrors happen during stages three and four of deep sleep, when no dreaming is taking place. Between one and two hours after going to bed, a child with night terrors will partially arouse from deep sleep and begin suddenly screaming, flailing, kicking, and sweating. Parents should not jar their child awake but carefully monitor the situation to make sure the child doesn't get hurt. A night terror may last for as little as half a minute or up to an hour. When it is over, the child falls back to sleep. Like sleepwalking, those who experience night terrors rarely remember them in the morning, though they may have a sense of fear upon awakening.

Sleep scientists say night-terror attacks can be reduced if children are gently awakened about fifteen minutes before the time they usually have the night terror and then go back to sleep. Scientists aren't sure why this works but one possible reason is that awakening a child right before a night terror gives the brain a chance to "practice" transitioning from one sleep stage to the next without the disruption of a night terror. As the brain develops, it learns how to smoothly flow from one sleep stage to the next. This is why sleep disorders such as night terrors and sleepwalking usually disappear by the time someone reaches puberty. Sleep scientists aren't sure exactly what causes sleepwalking or night terrors, but research has shown that both sleep disorders tend to run in families.

Obstructive sleep apnea is a serious, and potentially deadly, disorder in which someone briefly stops breathing during sleep at least five times each night. This may be due to a stuffed-up nose or the tongue or tonsils blocking the

Sleep Attacks

A rare sleep disorder called narcolepsy causes a person to unexpectedly fall asleep during the day. A sleep attack can last for a few minutes to several hours. It can hit anytime—while talking, shopping, or even driving. Two-thirds of narcolepsy patients also experience cataplexy, sudden muscle weakness in the body, while awake. This loss of muscle control, especially in the legs, face, and neck, is often triggered by emotional responses such as laughing. The first symptoms of narcolepsy are excessive sleepiness and cataplexy, and most frequently appear in young people between the ages of ten and twenty. Narcolepsy is incurable but can be managed with the proper medication.

Within the past few years, scientists have made major advances in narcolepsy research. They have linked the disorder to the lack of a chemical in the brain called hypocretin. It is hoped that new treatments to target this chemical may eliminate narcolepsy altogether.

airway. During an episode, which can last for ten seconds to a minute or more, no air enters the lungs. The sleeper struggles to breathe, briefly awakens, then goes back to sleep, never realizing or remembering what happened. The cycle may repeat hundreds of times during the night. Snoring is often a symptom of the disorder, though not everyone who snores has obstructive sleep apnea. Those who are over their target weight are more at risk for developing obstructive sleep apnea.

About seventy million American adults and children suffer from sleep disorders. Yet 95 percent of those who have a sleep disorder don't even know it.

The treatment of sleep problems and disorders costs Americans nearly $16 billion per year. Studies estimate that about seventy million American adults and children suffer from sleep disorders—that's one quarter of the population. Yet 95 percent of those who have a sleep disorder don't even know it. A person may feel exhausted all the time but not seek medical advice. Also, research has found that doctors might not be doing enough to spot sleep problems. In a survey of six hundred pediatricians (doctors who specialize in treating children), less than half took the time to question their adolescent patients about sleep habits.

Sleep disorders can be silent burglars, robbing you of sleep without you even being aware of what is happening. It is important not to ignore any of the warning signs. Here are a few questions to ask yourself:

- Does it take you more than thirty minutes to fall asleep?
- Do you frequently wake up during the night and have trouble going back to sleep?
- Do you have a hard time getting up in the morning?
- Do you rely on caffeinated beverages, like soda, tea, or coffee, to get you going in the morning?
- Do you "sleep in" for more than two hours on the weekend?
- When you wake up, are the blankets in disarray?
- Has someone told you that you snore, walk, or talk in your sleep?
- Do you fall asleep at school?

If you answered "yes" to any of the above questions, you may have a sleep problem. Try going to bed earlier and following the good sleep hygiene tips offered earlier in this chapter. If your symptoms continue, tell your parents and be sure to see your family doctor.

Now that you know the value of a good night's sleep, you are ready to take the next step. Let's travel into the foggy, mysterious world of dreams—a place where self-expression and imagination take flight.

Part Two
Dreams

Four

In Your Dreams

ntil the middle of the twentieth century, before the invention of EEGs, scientists were uncertain of the relationship between sleep and dreams. Were dreams simply fleeting images that passed before our eyes just before waking? Or did they indicate something more?

In the 1950s, University of Chicago professor and sleep scientist Nathaniel Kleitman and his colleague Eugene Aserinsky discovered REM sleep. Kleitman was watching his eight-year-old son sleeping and noticed something interesting. The child's eyes were moving quickly back and forth beneath his eyelids. Using newly developed EEG technology, Kleitman and

Aserinsky found that during this stage of sleep the brain was almost as active as when it was awake—a startling discovery. The researchers were certain that dreaming and REM sleep were connected, but they had to be sure. With the help of a young student named William Dement, who would later found the sleep disorder center at Stanford University, Kleitman and Aserinsky began conducting REM sleep experiments. Their research showed that when people were awakened during REM sleep, 80 to 95 percent of the sleepers could recall in amazing detail what they had just been dreaming.

Experts agree we can dream during any stage of sleep. Yet the dreams that occur in non-REM sleep appear to be less frequent, not as vivid, and more similar to the practical themes of real life. REM dreams, by contrast, are far more emotional, intense, and elaborate. They are also the ones we tend to remember. Some scientists suggest that rapid eye movement is how we observe what is occurring in a dream, which would explain why we have better recall of dreams that occur during this phase of sleep.

The Dream Seekers

For centuries, dreams have captivated even as they have be-wildered those who have tried to understand them. Many early civilizations looked to dreams for spiritual guidance. The Bible contains more than 120 references to dreams. One of the most well known is Jacob's dream of a ladder extending from Earth to heaven. Ancient Egyptians believed that dreams were messages or warnings from the gods. Anyone who wanted help from the gods would fall asleep in a temple so that a priest could later interpret their dreams. In Greece, a sick person would sleep in a holy temple hoping to receive a dream from the gods that would indicate health would soon be restored. Greek philosopher Aristotle (384–322 B.C.) was one of the first to suggest that dreams came from within the dreamer and were born from daily events.

Stone-Age Dreamers

The artistry discovered in prehistoric caves in Lascaux, France, indicates that people may have been recording their dreams as far back as 30,000 B.C. More than two thousand engravings and drawings of animals adorn the cave walls, yet only one drawing depicts a human. The painting shows a bird-headed man next to a stick, or staff, topped with a bird's head. Dream experts say the image likely represents a shaman, a religious leader who received spiritual guidance through dreams and visions.

The study of dreams took a leap forward in the early twentieth century with Austrian physician Sigmund Freud. In his book *The Interpretation of Dreams*, first published in

November 1899, Freud wrote that dreams came from the unconscious mind. He concluded that we have a conscious mind, or thoughts we are aware of, and an unconscious mind, or a collection of thoughts, desires, and emotions we aren't aware of but that influence how we behave.

Our unconscious mind, he felt, is the place where we push certain feelings we don't want to think about or act on during the day. He said that these thoughts, often rooted in childhood, couldn't be buried for long. They had to surface in the form of dreams. "A dream is the fulfillment of a wish," he claimed. Further, Freud suggested that many of the issues stewing in our unconscious mind revolve around violence and sex. Many of Freud's critics say his preoccupation with these themes had to do with living in the prim and proper Victorian era, a time when these subjects were considered taboo.

Carl Jung, a Swiss colleague of Freud's, shared many of his ideas but had a more upbeat view of dreams. Jung did not believe dreams hid our darkest thoughts and urges. Instead, he felt they were windows to our inner selves that should be welcomed and explored. In fact, Freud and Jung's bitter arguments over interpreting dreams eventually caused them to break off their relationship.

Today, most researchers agree that examining our dreams is a good way to learn more about ourselves. Yet there is often much debate over the reason why we dream.

Some experts say dreaming keeps the brain alert and healthy. Others believe dreams are a way to release stress and find solutions to problems. Dreams may also help us sort out our experiences and link new memories with those of the past. Or maybe we dream for the most obvious reason of all: to give our minds a creative outlet. Dreams are our chance to run wild and express the outrageous. Perhaps only in our dreams can we be truly and completely free.

Doing Your Dream Work

When searching your dreams for meaning, it is important to remember that no one has, or ever will have, a dream quite like yours. That is why the best dream interpreter is not a scientist, therapist, dream dictionary, or your best friend. It is *you.* You decide what your dreams mean and what they reveal about you.

Although each person's dreams are unique, as humans our dream tapestries tend to share a few common threads. We all argue with friends, worry about schoolwork, and wonder if a certain boy or girl will notice us. So it's not surprising that, because we share similar experiences, we also have

No one has, or ever will have, a dream quite like yours. That is why the best dream interpreter is you.

Common Dream Themes

Description	General Interpretation
Being chased or attacked	This indicates you may feel threatened or overwhelmed by a situation in your life. Being chased is a normal response to stress. It may signal the need for you to turn and face your "attacker" — meaning your problem — head-on.
Being loved	Dreams of hugging, kissing, and romance arise from our natural desire to be accepted and to have strong relationships with others. You may feel as if you're missing emotional support in your life.
Being injured or dying	If you or someone you love dies in a dream, it may mean you feel emotionally hurt or are coping with change. It does not mean that someone will die in real life — that is a myth.
Having teeth fall out	Having your teeth fall out in a dream may indicate you're angry and are having trouble expressing it. It may also mean you are insecure about a situation in your life. This is one of the most common injury dreams.
Flying	You have freedom in your life to achieve your goals. Are you flying away from something in your dream? Perhaps you want more freedom.

Description	General Interpretation
Failing a test or being embarrassed at school	It's normal to dream about failing a test, not being able to open your locker, or showing up to class in your underwear. This may signal that you feel ill prepared to cope with a challenge in life. Maybe you fear not being able to pass this "test." Being naked may mean you are afraid of revealing your true self to others.
Falling/drowning	Are you dealing with change in your life? If so, you may be insecure, uncomfortable, and uncertain about how to handle it. Perhaps you don't feel you have emotional support from others. Drowning may indicate you are feeling overwhelmed.
Interacting with celebrities/ athletes	The celebrity you dream about likely has qualities you admire and want to bring out in yourself, such as courage, style, or creativity. Do you dream that *you* are the celebrity, superhero, or athlete? You may be looking to accomplish a particular goal of your own.
Experiencing natural disasters	Experiencing an earthquake, tornado, or other catastrophic event may mean you are facing problems in life that you feel are spiraling out of control.
Being lost or trapped	Which way should you go? You don't know. Being lost in a maze, city, or forest is a common dream, indicating that you are unsure about how to deal with a particular issue.

some of the same types of dreams. Dreams are a nighttime extension of our daily lives. In them, we search for answers, struggle with issues, and set goals.

Eleven-year-old Justin had a dream in which he was riding a chairlift with his dad. "We were skiing, like we always do, and having fun," he remembers. "We were almost to the top of the mountain when a piece of the cable holding our chair snapped. As I was dangling in midair, my dad made it to the pole and climbed down the ladder. I tried to scream, but when I opened my mouth nothing came out. Below me, everything was completely black—like the sky at night without the moon. My gloves were slipping, and I knew I wasn't going to be able to hold on much longer. Nobody came to help me. I couldn't speak or yell. I lost my grip, and, as I was falling into the black sky, I woke up. Weird, huh?"

Actually, Justin's dream isn't that unusual. Studies show that falling is one of the most typical dreams people experience. Other frequent dream themes include being chased, flying, and failing a test or being embarrassed at school. Many of our most common dreams tend to focus on negative situations. This is because fear, sadness, anger, and anxiety are powerful emotions. They may remain at the forefront of our minds as we sleep, slipping into our melting pot of dreams.

The Language of Dreams

Dreams convey messages to us through pictures rather than words. Sound is present in about half of all dreams, while other senses like taste, touch, and smell occur in only a small percentage of dreams. Sometimes the meaning of a dream image may be quite obvious, or literal. Suppose, as you walk to school each day, you have to scurry past a Doberman that barks at you from behind a fence. At night, you dream that a dog attacks you. Clearly, you are concerned about having to deal with a scary situation each day. The message is a literal one because the dog in your dream stands for the dog in your waking life.

Frequently, though, the pictures in our dreams are figurative, or symbolic. A symbol is something that represents something else. Every day, you come across symbols in your waking life that you have learned the meaning of and no longer need to think about. A red traffic light is a symbol for—what? Stop, of course. Likewise, the characters, colors, and objects in our dreams stand for certain thoughts, emotions, and issues we are dealing with in our waking lives. For instance, seeing a bridge in a dream might signify it's time for a change; scissors could mean you want to cut off a stressful friendship; and an earthquake might indicate that you are ready to shake things up in your life.

Unlike life, where we must learn the meaning of symbols, in dreams, you decide what a particular symbol represents for you. There is no right or wrong answer. The same symbol will convey different things to different people. For instance, you might dream of being stuck in a dense fog. Perhaps you are trying to decide whether or not you have the time to play on a soccer team, so for you the fog symbolizes your uncertainty. On the other hand, weather forecasters who dream of fog may simply be taking their work to sleep.

Do-It-Yourself Dream Dictionary

Have you ever seen those cookie-cutter dream dictionaries that say things like: If a squirrel appears in your dream, you'll win the lottery? Instead of relying on a dream dictionary written by someone who will never experience your distinctive dreams, why not make your own? What does an airplane mean to you? How about a sports car, a bag of marshmallows, or a bouquet of red roses? Create a list of familiar objects you've already dreamed about (and ones you haven't). Write a few words about what each represents to you. As you recall your dreams, keep adding new symbols and meanings to your list. Save your personalized dream dictionary and keep it handy. It just might provide you with some valuable clues and insights as you record your dreams in a journal (see Chapter 5, "Dream Weaver").

How do you start decoding your dream symbols? "Look at your life," advises dream expert and psychotherapist, Joan Mazza. "You won't have to look very far. A dream is about something current. It's going to be about something you already know, something you're dealing with in your life." If you experience one of the more common dream themes listed on p. 46, use the suggested interpretations in the chart to start thinking about what your dream might be trying to convey. Can you make a connection between something in your dream and an issue you're facing in real life?

For Justin, several symbols made sense. His father had recently gotten transferred to a new job, which had up-rooted the family. At first, Justin had been excited about moving to a new state, but it had been difficult adapting to a new school. His classes were much harder and the kids weren't as friendly. This could account for why the chairlift ride in his dream had started out pleasantly but soon soured. Justin felt that the broken chairlift cable was a symbol that represented having to break off from his old friends and life. "I've tried to talk to my parents about everything, but they don't seem to understand how hard it's been for me," says Justin. "I guess that's why, in my dream, I couldn't scream and why my dad didn't help me." Justin's final fall into the black sky likely symbolized his feelings of helplessness.

A Dream Come True

In early April 1865, United States President Abraham Lincoln told a friend he had a dream where he heard people crying. He followed them into the east wing of the White House and saw his corpse in a coffin. On April 14, 1865, only a few nights after his vivid dream, Lincoln was assassinated by John Wilkes Booth at Ford's Theater in Washington, D.C. Lincoln's dream could be considered precognitive, or foretelling the future. Most dream experts say that precognitive dreams are rare, but they do happen.

In 1959, scientist Rita Dwyer was working in her lab developing rocket fuel when, without warning, the fuel exploded. Without hesitation, Dwyer's coworker, Ed Butler, rushed into the flames and pulled her to safety. Dwyer was severely burned in the accident but survived. Later, her rescuer revealed that, over the course of several years, he had been having a recurring nightmare about saving her from just such a fire. So accurate were the details of the dream that when the accident happened in real life, Butler thought he was dreaming. Once he realized it was real, Butler did exactly as he had done countless times in his sleep. "We were both so overwhelmed by it," remembers Dwyer, "that we didn't talk about it for a long time. We didn't tell anyone. We could hardly believe it ourselves."

Your Wildest Dreams

Sometimes the symbols in our dreams don't appear to have an obvious link to anything going on in our lives. In fact, they may seem ridiculous. "I dreamt I was knitting a glowing green sweater, but I couldn't seem to get the ball of yarn untangled," recalls Caroline, age twelve. "The more I tried to undo the knots, the tighter they got. Then my knitting needles turned into spaghetti noodles and the whole sweater fell apart in my lap. After that, a slice of strawberry cheesecake danced past me. I tried to take a bite, but it was twirling too fast."

When dream symbols seem confusing, try this exercise. Pick out one or two major symbols. At the top of a blank piece

Color Your Dream World

The hues and shades that paint our dreams can be dripping with meaning. So pay attention to the colors in your dreams, and decode them as you would any other symbol. Here are a few general tips on what some colors may mean:

White—hope, truth, snow, weddings

Yellow—peace, happiness, distrust, flowers, sunshine

Orange—power, assertiveness, pumpkins, autumn leaves

Red—passion, love, anger, violence, blood, cars

Blue—sadness, spirituality, water, sky

Green—envy, health, money, grass, nature

Black—fear, loneliness, uncertainty, evil, night, space

of paper, write or draw the symbol you want to decode. Below it, list some things you would normally associate with that person, place, color, or object. Don't erase anything. Let your ideas come tumbling out, no matter how silly they seem.

When you are finished, go back and review your list. Does anything jump out at you that you can connect to a real-life issue? Put a star next to it. If not, give it some time, add thoughts as they come to you, and try again later. You may not always be able to decode the symbol, but an item on your list will often make sense to you. Don't forget to add the symbol and meaning to your personal dream dictionary.

Caroline chose to decode the green sweater in her dream. Using the exercise, she was able to unlock the meaning of what she had first dismissed as simply a nonsense dream. "I realized I had been trying to compete with my older sister," she concludes. "Melanie is very talented and can do so many things really well, while the stuff I try never seems to work out. That's probably why the sweater fell apart in my dream." Remember the dancing cheesecake that Caroline loved but couldn't manage to eat? "I think my dream was telling me I'd be a lot happier—you know, get to eat the cheesecake—if I'd stop trying to prove that I was as good as my sister," she says. "I am just going to be myself and do the best I can."

The more you practice decoding symbols, the better you will get. Of course, not every symbol in every dream is going

Decoding Dream Symbols

Two symbols: green + sweater

Green	Sweater
Grass	Warm, comfy
Peas	Autumn frost
Green eggs & ham	Itchy wool
My eyes are green	I have tons of sweaters
Green light = go	Grandma knits sweaters
✓ Green with envy	✓ Melanie, my sister, knits & crochets
St. Patrick's Day	✓ I can't knit or crochet
✓ Melanie's favorite color is lime	My cat sleeps on my sweaters
Money	

to translate to a waking issue. Sometimes a dancing cheese-cake is just, well, a dancing cheesecake. Some symbols will immediately make sense to you, and some may never be clear—that's just how we dream. Also, don't feel you have to get to the heart of every single symbol in every single dream. You don't. Dream exploration should be exciting, engaging, and enlightening. But mostly, it should be fun.

Five

Dream Weaver

Among many Native American cultures of North America, such as the Chippewa, Lakota, Dakota, Cherokee, and Navajo, it is customary to make dream catchers. Designed to resemble a spider's web, threads are woven in a crisscross pattern across a twig hoop. Several strings trimmed with beads and feathers dangle beneath the circle. Each culture has a slightly different version of how the dream catcher works. For the most part, traditional legend holds that the ring allows good dreams to slip through the net, sliding down the feathers into the mind of the sleeper below. Nightmares become entangled in the web and are melted away by the rising sun. When the sleeper awakens, he or she sees the dream catcher and remembers only those dreams that were good.

Perhaps you, too, would like to "catch" and interpret some of your dreams. If so, a dream journal may help you to navigate and chart your nocturnal adventures of the mind. To begin, you will need a flashlight, a pad of paper, and a pen (or a tape recorder). You will also need a dream journal. A loose-leaf, three-ring binder with an inside pocket for your dream dictionary is a good choice. This will allow you to add pages continually to your dream journal.

Capturing Dreams

If you live to be eighty years old, you will have devoted more than five years to REM sleep. In that time, your mind will have spun hundreds of thousands of dream tapestries. Dream experts say we forget most of what we dream. What we do recall is rarely a complete story with a beginning, middle, and end. Instead, our minds jump from topic to topic. We are fortunate if we can snatch a few fragments of these images. Still, there are some things you can do to remember more of your dreams more often.

Before you go to sleep, place the flashlight, pad, and pen (or tape recorder) that you've gathered on a table beside your bed. As you lie back on your pillow, remind yourself that you want to recall your dream. Say, "I will remember what I dream." Do this a few times. It might seem strange, but it works. If you happen to wake up in the middle of the night with a dream in your head, keep your eyes closed and replay the dream a few times. Give it a temporary title and say it out loud so you'll remember. You may be tempted to fall back to sleep, sure that you will remember the dream in the morning. If you do this—if you go back to sleep—you will probably forget your dream by the next day. Once you have rehearsed your dream, open your eyes, turn on your flashlight, and write down the title and basic details. Don't try to edit anything or exaggerate to make the story better.

When you wake up in the morning take a moment to ask yourself, "What was I just dreaming?" Remember, we are most likely to recall what we were dreaming in our final REM cycle of the night. Write down on your notepad anything you can recall about your dream. Here are some questions to ask to help you get to the heart of the dream:

- What was the **story** in the dream? What happened?
- What was the **setting** of the dream? (home, school, library)
- Who were the **characters** in the dream?
- What was **I doing** in the dream?
- What was the **mood** of the dream? (scary, depressing, joyful)

When Good Dreams Go Bad

Most people have a really bad dream, called a nightmare, about once a month. Experts say nightmares are a wake-up call that there is a problem we need to attend to in our daily lives. So interpret your nightmares the same way you would any other dream. Nightmares may spring from stress, worries, a past traumatic event, medication, or illness. Ask yourself whether there is something going on in your life that's really bothering you. Once a problem is faced and handled in real life, the nightmare it sparked will usually disappear as well.

If you have a recurring nightmare (one that shows up on a regular basis), there are some things you can do to help stop it. "Try self-talk," advises sleep expert Dr. Jodi Mindell. "If you have a recurring nightmare that, say, a burglar is going to break in, tell yourself the facts—Mom and Dad are in the house, we have an alarm system, we have a big dog, people rarely break into houses. By talking to yourself, you can ease your fears as you go to bed." If you have a particularly violent nightmare or one that won't go away, tell your parents. You also might want to share it with a psychotherapist, a licensed professional trained in human behavior. "Therapy can be really helpful in teaching you how to cope and make you less anxious," says Mindell.

- What **objects** and **colors** were in my dream?
- How did the dream **end**? Or did it?
- How do I **feel** right now?

Don't try to interpret or decode anything yet. You'll do that later in your dream journal. For now, just focus on remembering as much as you can. If you're having trouble, try this: Lie in bed, relax, close your eyes, and work backward from where the dream ended to where it began. Also, you may find that as the day goes on, pieces of the dream come to mind. If so, write what you recall on a scrap of paper and tuck it in your pocket to take home. Don't be discouraged if, at first, you can only "catch" a tiny bit of your dream. Dream recall takes practice.

Bringing Dreams to Life

Once the first impressions of your dream are recorded on your notepad or tape recorder, you are ready to transfer everything to your dream journal. Perhaps you also have some scraps of paper you've scribbled notes on during the day. Gather everything together and turn to a fresh page in your dream journal.

Although you will want to title your dream, wait until after you have finished interpreting your dream. Then you can be sure that it accurately reflects the meaning of your dream.

First, using your notes, write the plot, or story, of your dream in the top third of the page. Beneath your description, on the left side of the page, list the settings, characters,

Dream Journal Entry

Date: Title:

Dream Story:

Symbols | My Interpretation

Setting(s):

Characters:

Main objects:

Moods & colors:

What is my dream saying to me?

If I could dream this dream again I would...

What action could I take in my waking life?

objects, moods, colors, and any important details you can remember. Across from each point, write down what you think each of these major symbols might represent. If there's a symbol you're not sure about or would like to investigate more deeply, go back to the decoding exercise on p. 53. Also, check your personal dream dictionary for hints as well. Remember, dreams communicate to us through pictures so feel free to draw in your dream journal. Be creative!

Finally, in the bottom third of the page, write what you feel the dream is saying to you. Look for connections between the symbols in your dream and the issues you are currently dealing with in your life. Ask yourself what choices you or others made in the dream. For instance, if you were being chased, did you run or did you confront your attacker? If you ran, perhaps there is a problem you are "running" from during the day, too. Some key questions to answer might be:

- What is this dream telling me? Is it helping me to solve a problem or set a goal?
- If I could dream this dream again, what would I do differently?
- Could I take some sort of action in my waking life?

At last, you are ready to give your dream a title. To get an idea of how a complete entry in your dream journal might look, see the dream thirteen-year-old Amy called "What's Bugging Me?"

Amy's Dream Journal

Date: December 10th   **Title:** What's Bugging Me?

Dream Story: My friends Breanne, Sarah, and I are in my kitchen making popcorn. Some of the kids from my computer class at school show up. I don't want them to come in, but Bree does so we invite them inside. They drop popcorn all over the floor, and spill pop on the carpet. I tell them I'm going to get in trouble with my parents, but they only laugh. When the microwave "dings" I open the door to take out another bag of popcorn and, suddenly, a whole bunch of big, black beetles and spiders pour out of the microwave. It's really gross. They are everywhere. The kitchen is filled with thousands of bugs. I scream and run! The scene switches to my school. I am racing down the stairs but when I get to the bottom there is no door. It's just a cement wall. I can't get out. The dream ends with me trapped at the bottom of the stairs. I am scared because I know I am not going to escape the bugs.

Symbols	My Interpretation
Setting(s):	
My House	I feel relaxed and safe at my house.
School	I like school, except for computer class.
Characters:	
Breanne, Sarah, & Me	I usually have fun with my friends.
Kids from computer class	I am uncomfortable. They are intruders.
Main objects:	
Popcorn	My favorite snack, fun to make with my friends
Bugs	Scary, creepy, "computer bug" (problems)
Stairwell with no exit	Trapped, helpless, alone

Amy's Dream Journal (Continued)

<u>Symbols</u> *(Continued)*	<u>My Interpretation</u> *(Continued)*

Moods & Colors:
Happy when making
  popcorn
Nervous when the kids
  show up
Frightened when the
  bugs attack
Bugs were black and
  shiny
	When I am with my friends I
	  feel good.
	I feel stressed-out in computer
	  class
	Bugs scare me.
	Once, a daddy longlegs crawled
	over my neck
	when we were
	camping!!

What is my dream saying to me?
I am behind in my computer class, and trying to catch up. Sometimes, the teacher goes too fast, but I don't say anything. It doesn't help that the kids who sit in my group talk all the time, and hardly do any work. They don't care if I fail. But I do. I think the dream is telling me that the class and these people are really "bugging" me. I know that if things stay the way they are, it's only going to get worse for me in class.

If I could dream this dream again I would...
Kick the kids out of my house when they start acting up and spilling things. I would squash the bugs, instead of running from them.

What action could I take in my waking life?
I could talk to my computer teacher. I could tell him I am having a hard time and ask for extra help to catch up. Also, I could ask to be moved away from the noisy kids to a quieter area of the room.

As your dream journal begins to take shape, you will find it interesting to look back at your old dreams. Perhaps some of the same characters and themes crop up again and again. These recurring items no doubt represent your friends, family, schoolmates, and routine activities in which you are involved. Some dreams might not make sense to you until much later. Others may never be unraveled at all, and that's OK. Even if you only capture a few dreams, you will be on your way to discovering more about yourself.

Changing Your Destiny?

Is it possible to choose what you dream about or even alter parts of your dream the way you might write a story? Some dream experts think so. Dream incubation is the practice of asking your mind to give you a dream about a specific subject. Incubating dreams was popular in ancient Egypt, Italy, and Greece, as people sought guidance through their dreams. Today, people often use dream incubation to try to "dream up" the solution to a particular problem or issue. Does it work? Chances are pretty good that if you are thinking about a certain topic as you go to sleep—especially something that puzzles you—your mind is likely to mull it over in your dreams.

Writers often fall asleep wondering what direction their stories should take only to have the answer revealed in a dream. English writer Charlotte Brontë, author of *Jane Eyre,*

Chances are pretty good that if you are thinking about a certain topic as you go to sleep—especially something that puzzles you—your mind is likely to mull it over in your dreams.

often went to bed willing herself to dream about her plots and characters. Nineteenth-century Russian chemist Dmitry Mendeleyev spent years trying to come up with a way to classify chemical elements. Finally, one night he dreamed of a pattern in which all the elements line up according to atomic weight, and the periodic table of elements was born. Experts say that dreaming a solution to a problem isn't uncommon. It may be that our minds are too distracted during the day, dealing with normal tasks such as schoolwork, meeting with friends, and other activities. At night, however, the mind is able to relax. Once the underbrush of our daily lives is cleared away, the path we should take may become obvious.

Have you ever been dreaming and, suddenly, it occurs to you that you are, in fact, in the middle of a dream? This is called lucid dreaming. It usually happens by accident. You may be having a normal dream when you realize, "Hey, wait, I'm dreaming." True lucid dreaming happens rarely, though dream researchers say some people can train themselves to do it. In theory, a lucid dream may allow the dreamer to take control of the story, to change details or alter the ending. Lucid dreaming is sometimes useful in therapy to help those who are struggling with recurrent nightmares, such as Vietnam veterans or trauma victims. By standing up to their fears and changing how they react in a bad dream, people may be able to put their recurring nightmares to bed once and for all.

The Dream Mirror

Throughout the ages, dreams have inspired artists, poets, musicians, filmmakers, architects, and scientists. Great minds, such as composer Wolfgang Mozart, artist Pablo Picasso, scientist Albert Einstein, and playwright William Shakespeare, have attributed some of their most amazing creations to the powerful impact of dreams.

In the 1920s, people became fascinated by the exploration of dreams and the unconscious mind, forming what is known as the surrealist movement. Heavily influenced by the ideas of Sigmund Freud, surrealism found its way into the books, art, and films of the early twentieth century. Spanish surrealist painter Salvador Dalí called his works "hand-painted dream photographs." Dalí would often nap during the day clutching a paintbrush. When he awoke, he would immediately set to work capturing on canvas the images that had just floated through his dreams.

"There is a magical mirror in this place we find ourselves while dreaming," said noted dream researcher Dr. Montague

Ullman, founder of the Dream Laboratory at Maimonides Medical Center in Brooklyn, New York. In a speech titled "Dreams as Exceptional Human Experiences," Ullman told an audience, "It is a mirror capable of reflecting a profoundly honest picture of who we are, rather than who we would like to think we are or who we would like others to think we are."

Dreams reflect our unspoken thoughts, deepest fears, and greatest hopes. Yet they are as elusive as wispy clouds, slipping through our fingers even as we reach out for them. Perhaps it is this haunting, untouchable nature that keeps us spellbound. Each night, we travel down a winding road never quite knowing where it will lead but certain it will reveal a little bit more about who we are. So we follow the path. And we dream on.

Glossary

biological clock: an area of your brain that controls the sleep-wake cycle and other circadian rhythms (see SCN); also called your body clock

brain waves: tiny electrical charges continually emitted by the brain while awake (beta waves) and during sleep (alpha, delta, and theta waves)

circadian rhythms: natural bodily functions such as the sleep-wake cycle, body temperature, heart rate, and blood pressure that follow a repetitive daily cycle

coma: a state of unconsciousness from which a person cannot be awakened; characterized by brain waves that are slow and barely detectable

dream catcher: a traditional Native American craft patterned after a spider's web with threads woven across a twig hoop; legend says the dream catcher captures good dreams and keeps nightmares away

dream incubation: the practice of asking your mind to give you a dream about a specific subject before you go to sleep

electroencephalograph (EEG): a device that amplifies and records the electrical charges given off by the brain; the written record of brain-wave patterns is called an electroencephalogram

human growth hormone: a natural chemical released during sleep that repairs cells and tissues and that stimulates growth and development

insomnia: difficulty falling or staying asleep; short-term insomnia may be the result of stress, diet, or poor sleep hygiene, while prolonged insomnia may be a symptom of a sleep disorder

lucid dreaming: becoming aware while dreaming that you are, in fact, in a dream

melatonin: a natural chemical produced by the brain that causes a person to feel sleepy microsleep: brief periods of sleep in an otherwise awake individual lasting from a few seconds to several minutes

narcolepsy: a rare sleep disorder primarily characterized by unexpectedly falling asleep during the day and sudden attacks of muscle weakness called cataplexy

nightmare: a bad dream that often has a violent theme, which may awaken its dreamer

night terrors: a sleep disorder occurring in the deepest stage of sleep in which a person awakens, screams and thrashes wildly for a brief period of time, and then falls back to sleep

non-REM sleep: the first four stages of sleep, including deep or slow-wave sleep

obstructive sleep apnea: a potentially deadly sleep disorder in which a person briefly stops breathing during sleep; caused by a blockage in the airway

pineal gland: a pea-size organ in the brain that produces (or stops producing) melatonin based on signals it receives from the SCN

REM sleep (rapid eye movement): the stage of sleep character-ized by increased brain activity and vivid dreaming; we are most likely to recall our dreams if awakened during REM sleep

seasonal affective disorder (SAD): a medical condition caused by lack of sufficient sunlight characterized by depression, mood swings, lack of energy, weight gain, and isolation

sleep: a state of partial or full unconscious rest from which you can be awakened

sleep cycle: a loop of five stages that occurs during sleep; we pass through the sleep cycle about five times each night

sleep debt: the difference between the amount of sleep your body needs to feel well rested and the amount of sleep you actually get; sleep debt accumulates over time and may result in serious fatigue-related mistakes if not repaid

sleep deprivation: a lack of sufficient sleep, which may alter mood and result in errors in judgment

sleep disorder: a persistent problem with sleep that affects the sleep-wake cycle and a person's ability to function adequately during the day

sleep-wake cycle: the human body's natural, repetitive pattern of sleeping and waking; a circadian rhythm regulated by the body's internal clock and external forces, such as sunlight

sleepwalking: a sleep disorder that occurs during slow-wave sleep characterized by the sleeper partially awakening to sit up or move around

slow-wave sleep: the deepest level of sleep where scientists say the body gets its most thorough rest as it recharges and repairs for the day ahead; also called deep sleep

suprachiasmatic nucleus (SCN): an area of the brain, also known as the biological clock, which regulates circadian rhythms such as the sleep-wake cycle, body temperature, heart rate, and blood pressure

Further Resources

Books

Bayer, Linda. *Sleep Disorders.* Philadelphia: Chelsea House, 2000.

Garfield, Patricia. *The Dream Book.* Toronto, Ontario: Tundra Books, 2002.

McPhee, Andrew T. *Sleep and Dreams.* Danbury, Conn.: Franklin Watts, 2001.

Policoff, Stephen Phillip. *The Dreamer's Companion: A Young Person's Guide to Understanding Dreams and Using Them Creatively.* Chicago: Chicago Review Press, 1997.

Shaw, Tucker. *Dreams.* New York: Penguin Putnam, 2000.

Simpson, Carolyn. *Coping with Sleep Disorders.* New York: Rosen Publishing Group, 1996.

Online Sites and Organizations

Association for the Study of Dreams
P.O. Box 1166
Orinda, CA 94563
www.asdreams.org
This nonprofit organization is devoted to encouraging dream research and promoting awareness of dream study. The ASD Web site offers answers to the most common dream questions, tips on how to interpret your own dreams, and school science projects.

National Sleep Foundation
1522 K St. NW
Suite 500
Washington, D.C. 20005
www.sleepfoundation.org
The nonprofit National Sleep Foundation works to improve health and safety by educating the public about sleep deprivation and disorders. Think you know all about sleep? Take an online quiz to test your sleep IQ, and take a survey to find out how well you are sleeping.

National Center on Sleep Disorders Research

National Institutes of Health

Two Rockledge Center, Ste. 10038

6701 Rockledge Dr., MSC 7920

Bethesda, MD 20892

www.nhlbi.nih.gov/about/ncsdr

This government organization is dedicated to studying sleep disorders, training professionals in the medical field, and educating the public. At the Web site, you can find in-depth information on sleep disorders such as chronic insomnia, narcolepsy, sleepwalking, and sleep apnea.

Neuroscience for Kids

Dept. of Psychology

University of Washington

Seattle, WA 98195

faculty.washington.edu/chudler/chsleep.html

Explore how your brain and nervous system works at this easy-to-understand, visual site designed especially for young people. View charts of REM and non-REM brain waves, and compare your sleep needs to that of various animals.

Index

About the Author

Trudi Strain Trueit is an award-winning health and medical broadcast journalist. As a news reporter for KREM-TV (CBS) in Spokane, Washington, her weekly on-air segment, *Your Health,* earned recognition from the Society of Professional Journalists. *Unborn Ethics,* a documentary examining the controversy over genetic engineering, received top national honors from United Press International.

Her other titles in the Life Balance series include *ADHD* and *Eating Disorders.* Also a television weather forecaster, Trueit has written more than fifteen books for Scholastic about nature, weather, and wildlife. She has a degree in broadcast journalism, and lives in Everett, Washington, with her husband, Bill.

Special thanks to Dr. Jodi Mindell, associate professor of psychology at St. Joseph's University in Philadelphia, Pennsylvania, and Dr. Judith Owens, associate professor of pediatrics at Brown University School of Medicine and director of the Pediatric Sleep Disorders Clinic at Hasbro Children's Hospital in Providence, Rhode Island.